THE
fruit
COOKBOOK

THE
fruit
COOKBOOK

Jenny Stacey

SMITHMARK

This edition published in 1995 by
SMITHMARK Publishers Inc.,
16 East 32nd Street,
New York, NY 10016

1 3 5 7 9 8 6 4 2

SMITHMARK books are available for bulk purchase for sales promotion
and premium use. For details write or call the manager of special sales,
SMITHMARK Publishers Inc.,
16 East 32nd Street,
New York, NY 10016;
(212) 532-6600.

ISBN 0-8317-3467-1

CREDITS

COMMISSIONING EDITOR: *Will Steeds*
EDITOR: *Alison Leach*
DESIGN: *Carole Perks*
PHOTOGRAPHER: *Sue Jorgensen*
HOME ECONOMIST: *Nicola Fowler*
STYLIST: *Maria Kelly*
COLOR SEPARATION: *P & W Graphics*

Printed in Singapore

ABOUT THE INGREDIENTS

As seasoning is a matter of personal taste, salt and pepper are not
necessarily listed in the ingredients.
Try to obtain the best quality fresh produce.

Contents

❦

Author's Introduction

To wander through a market laden with fruit stalls, or to explore the fruit counters of supermarkets and specialty stores is now an exciting and hunger-inducing experience. In the past, due to the lack of suitable transportation and storage facilities, fruits were mostly limited to those grown in our respective countries, and supplies were very much dictated by the short seasons.

With the advance of technology we are now treated to a marvelous and ever-increasing choice in the varieties of fruits available throughout the year, allowing us to become more adventurous in our cooking, and to enjoy a feast of flavors formerly denied to our palates.

With the rapidly growing emphasis on health issues and healthy eating, fruit is now recognized as an essential part of our diets, providing variety in flavor, texture and, more importantly, low-calorie, enjoyable nutrients to keep us fit and healthy. Fruit should form a large part of our everyday diet, and fortunately this is easily achieved owing to its versatility.

Throughout this book I have tried to provide exciting recipes to suit every palate and budget, with dishes to suit every occasion, whether a quick snack, a family meal, or a formal dinner party.

Although their shelf life is relatively short, with a little planning we should all be able to make more use of fruits in our cooking, and take advantage of this unsurpassed food in our everyday diets. If fresh fruits are not available, canned or frozen fruits can sometimes be substituted. I hope that after trying some of the recipes in the following chapters, you will feel that I have helped you to appreciate just how invaluable fruit is as an ingredient, in addition to being eaten in its natural form.

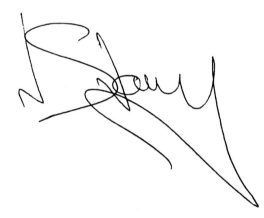

The History of Fruit

According to the book of Genesis, apples were the first fruit of the world, and immediately found to be irresistible. There is some dispute as to whether this is indeed true, some people saying that it may have been bananas that grew in the Garden of Eden. The banana, even if it were not the first fruit of the world, was certainly the first to be cultivated. Bananas were imported from the Canaries in 1882. With the advent of refrigerated ships early in the 20th century, bananas were exported from Bermuda. The fruits were much larger than those from the Canaries, which were sweeter.

The small, sweet apricot originates in China and Armenia. The US is now a leading world producer, and it is also grown in Asia and in southern Europe.

Black, red and white currants were first cultivated in the 17th century, although the black and white varieties did not enjoy a favorable reception in many parts of the world, due to their somewhat less appealing appearance. Other berries, such as the blueberry, native to North America, although popular in their country of origin, have also been fairly slow to become appreciated in other areas of the world.

There is some dispute over the origin of kiwi fruit, also known as the Chinese gooseberry, although there appears to be no mention of its use or existence in any Chinese recipes at all! New Zealand, however, acquired the first seeds from China, and now it is one of the country's major exports, and it has become one of the most commonly used "exotic" fruits around the world.

Grapefruit are synonymous with Florida where they were first recognized in the 1830s, although not launched commercially until the 1880s. They are now grown throughout southern Europe as well as in the US.

As far as exotic fruits are concerned, the mango is perhaps one of the most familiar examples. It originated in India, although it is now also grown in Brazil and South Africa. The mango is grown on a small scale in the US. Pineapples were once considered to be a luxury. They were first imported from the West Indies in the 1870s, and are now one of the most popular fruits.

It is difficult to trace the origin of oranges as there are so many varieties. Oranges are now widely grown throughout the Mediterranean region, and, in the US, in Florida, California, and Texas but these are not their places of origin.

In 17th-century Europe, oranges became a symbol of prosperity, with the wealthy going to great lengths to protect their trees. Even today, orange trees are handed down through generations. The kumquat, a member of the orange family, is a fruit that without doubt originated in China, as did the tangerine.

Another contender to being the very first fruit on this earth is the grape. Grown on Mount Ararat, it is considered to be one of the earliest cultivated plants, its main purpose being to make wine. It seems that several fruits are vying for the title of "first fruit of the world," but whichever one qualifies, the popularity of fruits has not diminished through the centuries.

Cooking with Fruits

Fruits have undergone many technological changes in modern times, to aid the prevention of disease, and to produce higher yields and longer seasons. Keeping qualities have been improved, albeit with the use of chemicals. Although this is something that preferably would not be necessary, it has enabled fruits to be grown and exported around the world, allowing us to sample fruits that would otherwise be unavailable.

Technology has also made it possible for fruits to be available in the stores all year round, and has almost eliminated the seasons as we used to know them. Today fruits are packed before ripening, held in storage until they are required, and put through a ripening process so as to produce good-quality ripe fruits on our supermarket shelves throughout the year.

Fruit is one of the most important food commodities available. Being very nutritious, it provides us with essential vitamins and minerals required to keep us healthy. As it is low in calories, it is one food group that may be eaten in abundance without risking our health or piling on the pounds. Being readily available, there is no excuse for it not being eaten raw or used in our cooking as much as possible.

Most fruits are inexpensive, allowing even those on a tight budget to provide a healthy diet for their families. Quick to prepare and cook, fruits may be used in all manner of ways in both sweet and savory dishes, and may be used in combination with or in place of vegetables in many recipes to help to stretch more expensive ingredients.

An Introduction to Fruits

Apples

There are over 3000 named varieties of apple from sweet eating apples to tart cooking apples. Whether red or green, each apple has a distinctive flavor, the red shiny-skinned apples perhaps being less popular due to their tougher skin.

Apples should be bought a couple of days before being eaten in order that they have time to ripen at home. If picking your own, they should be wrapped in newspaper, and stored in stacks of wooden trays.

During preparation apples discolor very quickly, and should be tossed in lemon juice if it is required for flavoring, or placed in a bowl of lightly salted water, and rinsed just prior to use.

When buying apples, look for shiny, unblemished skins without any soft or brown patches. Always wash apples or peel them before eating.

Apricots

An early summer fruit with an unfortunately short season. There are so many varieties of apricot that it is impossible to choose between them. Select firm, ripe fruits. Generally the stronger the color, the sweeter the fruit. If required for cooking and not eating raw, the paler apricots are excellent, and may be used for pies, stuffings, soufflés and jams. In Middle Eastern cooking they are frequently combined with lamb.

Bananas

The green bananas are best used for cooking, and are usually boiled or fried, whereas the yellow bananas have a mellower, sweeter flavor. When buying, look for a good color with a few brown streaks on the skin. Store in a cool place, and eat within 2–3 days of purchase.

Bananas are a very versatile fruit, being combined with cheeses, figs, hams and meats, coconut, and, of course, rum to make a wide variety of dishes. The banana's greatest allies are lemons and limes, these being essential not only in preventing it from discoloring, but also combining well with its flavor.

Cherries

We all love the dark richness of cherries, the most popular being the morello. When buying cherries, always ask to taste them first to discover how sweet and juicy they really are. There are also sweet dessert cherries and cooking cherries, which tend to have more character. They are ideal when combined with almonds, and are often used as a delicious sauce to accompany meats and poultry. Their main drawbacks are their incredibly short season and the dreaded pits. Cherries should always be pitted before use in cooking; may we bless the inventor of that handy gadget, the cherry pitter!

Grapefruit

Again there are many varieties, including pink or ruby grapefruit. With its sweeter, succulent flesh, this has become very popular.

All grapefruit is best eaten raw, or very quickly and gently cooked. They are excellent with watermelon, avocado and cheeses, as well as being delicious in marmalade when combined with other citrus fruits. The thick skins are often candied for use as decoration.

When buying grapefruit, look for unblemished skins. They should feel heavy in the hand if ripe and juicy.

Grapes

There are basically black, green and red varieties, both seeded and seedless. After the skin is removed, there is very little difference in flavor and appearance between them. When buying grapes, look for quality, the better ones being presented in paper netting. Always ask to taste grapes before you buy them, and wash them thoroughly.

They are widely used in cooking with cheeses and meats, and as decoration.

Kiwi Fruit

This is not the most attractive of fruits in its natural state, having a green, hairy, thin skin. The flesh is bright green with a central core of dark seeds. A great advantage is its tolerance of storage, being able to be kept in a cool place for up to 8 weeks.

Widely used in combination with other exotic fruits, the kiwi fruit is often sliced and used as an attractive decoration for tarts, meringues and cheesecakes. A good way to enjoy a kiwi fruit is to treat it as a boiled egg and consume its fragrant flesh with a small spoon.

Lemons and Limes

These two fruits are talked about together as many of their characteristics are the same. Limes may be stored for longer than lemons, but when buying avoid wrinkled skins. The peel, after washing, is an asset to many recipes, imparting a mild citrus flavor. It is best removed finely, with a zester.

Both are used with many other fruits as a flavor enhancer, being excellent with meats and poultry, and essential with avocado and other tropical fruits. They are used to counteract the richness of fried and "heavy" foods.

Mangoes

Mangoes are still considered a luxury item. Their golden yellow skin hides a spectacular deep orange flesh, which has a slightly acidic, sweet flavor. Widely used in cooking, mangoes are suitable for ice creams, sorbets, chutneys, curries and as a dramatic decoration for puddings and desserts. The most efficient way to remove the flesh is to stand the mango on its end, and to cut from top to bottom on either side of the pit. The two sides may then be removed, and the pit discarded.

Melons

All melons should feel heavy in the hand in proportion to their size. Ripe melons will be softer at the stalk end, and have a pleasant scent. To prepare, cut melons in half, and scoop out the seeds, which, incidentally, may be dried and toasted, and eaten on their own.

Melons vary in size and flavor from large watermelons with bright pink flesh, through the green-fleshed Ogen to the pale and less dramatic honeydew with its mild color and flavor. Melons are used with meats, in mousses and ices, and are often combined with ginger, a flavor that complements the fruit well.

Pineapples

Pineapples may be used as containers for sweet and savory fillings, sliced and served with a flavored cream, added to fruit salads and stir-fries, or simply eaten raw. They do not freeze well, and are impossible to set with gelatin, although simmering first may help.

When buying, look at the plume of leaves. If they are a good color, and look fresh, the pineapple is fresh. When ripe, the leaves may be plucked from the plume with ease.

Cooking Methods

Fruits provide great inspiration for any cook, being suitable for most cooking methods.

Baking Mainly restricted to larger fruits such as apples and pears, although bananas may also be successfully baked. Often the fruits are used as containers for stuffings. Berries may also be baked with crisp crumble or biscuit toppings, or fruits may be baked *en papillote*.

Deep-frying Few fruits are suitable for deep-frying, as they break up in the intense heat. Fruits should be cut into even-sized pieces so as to cook evenly, fried quickly, and drained on paper towels before serving. Moist fruits should be dried before coating in batter, as the batter will not stick to them successfully otherwise.

Broiling Bananas, pineapples, apples, pears and peaches are ideal for broiling, which is a fast and efficient method of cooking. Fruits may be sliced or cut into chunks, and threaded onto kebab skewers, or baked whole with a little butter and a few spices.

Microwaving An excellent method of cooking fruits, they tend to hold their shape better, and retain much of their color, so look more appealing.

If a soft purée is required, the fruit should be cooked for a few minutes longer than specified in the recipe. A wide variety of fruits may be cooked in the microwave quickly, and eaten hot or cold, or used as a base for other dishes.

Firm-fleshed fruits should be pricked with a fork to prevent bursting. Skins do not need to be removed from fruits prior to cooking, as they are easily removed after being cooked in a microwave.

Poaching This is the simplest method of cooking as far as preparation is concerned. Stewed fruits are commonly served hot or cold, or used as a basis for a more adventurous dish.

Juicy, firm fruits should be picked, prepared and cut into even-sized pieces before cooking. Fruits may be poached in sugar syrups or in salted water. The lower the sugar content of the syrup, the faster the fruit will cook.

Steaming A quick and delicious method of cooking fruits, it retains color, texture, and importantly, nutrients. A whole apple only takes about 7–9 minutes to cook, oranges and peaches taking even less time. Steaming is one of the oldest methods of cooking, and is increasing in popularity due to its health advantages.

Fruit changes in consistency more than any other foodstuff in the freezer. The juicier the fruit, the softer it becomes on thawing, therefore freezing is not suitable for some fruits. Melons and bananas, for example, do not freeze successfully. Fruits are usually frozen either in syrup, in dry packs or as a purée. They should be frozen in rigid containers, usually with sugar. Allow 2 cups sugar for 3 pounds of fruit. Most fruits are best frozen sliced or puréed, but berries and currants are excellent open-frozen, and then packed into suitable containers. They generally last well for anything from 6 to 12 months.

Nutrition

Fruits are one of the most important foods that we eat, full of the essential vitamins and minerals required for our health and growth. Rich in Beta carotene, vitamin C, potassium, calcium and sodium, all fruits are packed with goodness. In general, they are low in calories, low (or have no) fat (except avocados), are free of cholesterol, and are fair-to-good sources of fiber. In addition, dried fruits are excellent sources of iron.

Apples, one of the most popular fruits in the world, are high in pectin, potassium, vitamin C and phosphorous, as are apricots which are also a good source of magnesium and iron.

Bananas contain more carbohydrate than other fruits, and are therefore not ideal for those on a diet. They are high in potassium, zinc, iron, folic acid, calcium and vitamin B6.

Blackberries and currants are an excellent source of vitamin C, as are citrus fruits, although limes contain less than lemons. Oranges are not only a rich source of vitamin C, but also many minerals. The kiwi fruit is another rich source of vitamin C, being equal to oranges in this respect.

Grapes have the highest sugar content of all the fruits, making them a useful addition to more acidic fruits.

Melons are an excellent fruit for those who are dieting, as their water content is 94 percent.

So it seems that the old saying "an apple a day keeps the doctor away" is not simply an old wives' tale, but a sensible piece of advice that should be heeded by all.

Hints and Tips

☙ Use lemon juice to prevent discoloration of non-acidic fruits such as apples, pears and bananas.

☙ Pour boiling water onto fruits and let sit for 5 minutes. The skins then peel away easily.

☙ Soak fruits such as oranges and lemons in hot water before juicing. The resulting yield will be far greater.

☙ Place whole fruits in the refrigerator to chill before peeling. The peel will then come away more easily.

☙ Make sauces from fruits, and freeze to produce quick and easy meals.

☙ Add a little salt to fruits to draw the flavor from them during cooking.

☙ To obtain a tight seal on jams, dampen the seals before placing on the jars, and they will tighten as the seal dries out.

☙ To test if a jam has set, drop a little onto a cold saucer. When a skin has formed, push gently with a finger, and the jam should wrinkle.

☙ Keep cut fruit fresh by covering the exposed area with waxed paper and then a glass container.

☙ Place lemons in a glass jar, and fill with water; seal and store to keep firm.

Soups & Appetizers

Recipes containing fruit make excellent appetizers, be they soups or pâtés, used in stuffings or in fruit cocktails. Freshening the palate in readiness for the forthcoming meal, fruit adds a unique flavor and texture to recipes, without being filling and so spoiling the appetite.

Chilled Mixed Fruit Soup

☙

3 tablespoons BUTTER
⅓ cup ALL-PURPOSE FLOUR
5 cups VEGETABLE STOCK
1¼ pounds MIXED FRUITS, SUCH AS RASPBERRIES, CHERRIES, BLACKBERRIES AND STRAWBERRIES
2½ cups LIGHT CREAM
juice of 1 LEMON
1 teaspoon GROUND CINNAMON

To garnish
LIGHT CREAM
MINT SPRIGS

Melt the butter in a pan, and add the flour. Cook for 1 minute. Remove from the heat, and stir in the stock and fruits gradually. Bring to a boil, then reduce the heat, and simmer for 10 minutes. Let cool slightly, then place in a food processor. Blend for 30 seconds, and strain into a bowl. Stir in the cream, lemon juice and cinnamon. Cover and chill for 3–4 hours.

Remove from the refrigerator, and spoon into individual serving dishes. Swirl in a little cream, and garnish with mint sprigs. SERVES 4

Celery & Apple Soup

☙

2 tablespoons BUTTER
1 ONION, CHOPPED
¼ cup ALL-PURPOSE FLOUR
6 CELERY STALKS, WASHED, TRIMMED AND SLICED
5 cups VEGETABLE STOCK
2 RED EATING APPLES, PEELED, CORED AND DICED
2 tablespoons SNIPPED FRESH CHIVES
⅔ cup LIGHT CREAM
SALT AND PEPPER
CELERY LEAVES, TO GARNISH

Melt the butter in a pan. Add the onion, and sauté for 5 minutes. Stir in the flour, and cook for an additional minute. Add the celery and stock, then season well. Bring to a boil, then reduce the heat, and simmer for 10 minutes. Stir in the apples and chives, and cook for an additional 10 minutes. Remove from the heat, and let cool slightly. Put the mixture into a food processor, reserving a few pieces of apple and celery. Blend the soup until smooth. Return to the pan, and add the reserved pieces of fruit and celery. Stir in the cream, and heat through. Serve garnished with celery leaves. SERVES 4

Top: Chilled Mixed Fruit Soup
Bottom: Celery & Apple Soup

Crab Melts

❧

3 cups WHITE CRABMEAT
1 tablespoon WORCESTERSHIRE SAUCE
1 teaspoon PAPRIKA
grated zest and juice of 1 LIME
¼ cup RED SEEDLESS GRAPES, CHOPPED
⅓ cup COOKED LONG-GRAIN AND WILD RICE
1 teaspoon PREPARED MUSTARD
1 RED BELL PEPPER, SEEDED AND DICED
1 tablespoon SNIPPED FRESH CHIVES
½ cup FRESHLY GRATED CHEDDAR CHEESE

Mix together the crabmeat and Worcestershire sauce in a bowl. Add the paprika, lime juice, zest and grapes. Stir in the cooked rice, mustard and bell pepper. Add the chives, and spoon into 4 scallop shells.

Top with the cheese, and cook under a medium-hot broiler for 5–7 minutes, or until the cheese has melted. Serve immediately. SERVES 4

Plum & Almond Soup

❧

1 pound DESSERT PLUMS, WASHED
1 tablespoon BUTTER
2 tablespoons ALL-PURPOSE FLOUR
3¾ cups VEGETABLE STOCK
1 teaspoon ALMOND EXTRACT
⅔ cup NATURAL YOGURT
grated zest and juice of 1 ORANGE
SALT AND PEPPER

To garnish
SLIVERED ALMONDS
CHOPPED FRESH CILANTRO

Halve the plums, and remove the pits. Chop the flesh into small pieces. Melt the butter in a large pan, and add the flour, then cook for 1 minute. Remove from the heat, and stir in the stock and plums. Season well. Add the almond extract, then return the pan to the heat, and cook for 20 minutes until the plums are soft. Press through a strainer, and let cool.

When cool, stir in the yogurt, orange zest and juice. Pour into individual serving bowls, and garnish. SERVES 4

Shrimp, Apple & Melon Cocktail

❧

1 RED EATING APPLE, WASHED
1 GREEN EATING APPLE, WASHED
2 tablespoons LEMON JUICE
½ HONEYDEW MELON, SEEDED AND PEELED
⅔ cup FROMAGE FRAIS
1 tablespoon TOMATO PASTE
few drops of TABASCO
few leaves of LOLLO ROSSO LETTUCE
8 ounces SHELLED TIGER SHRIMPS

Core and dice the apples, then toss in the lemon juice. Slice the melon, and cut the slices in half through the center.

Mix together the fromage frais, tomato paste and Tabasco. Arrange the melon on a plate with the lettuce. Mix the apples and shrimps together, and spoon onto the plate. Top with the sauce, and serve. SERVES 4

TOP: Crab Melts (left); Plum & Almond Soup (right)
BOTTOM: Shrimp, Apple & Melon Cocktail

Stuffed Mushrooms

☙

4 OPEN CAP MUSHROOMS

⅓ cup BROWN RICE

⅓ cup FRESH PINEAPPLE, PEELED, CORED AND CHOPPED

2 SCALLIONS, TRIMMED AND SLICED

1 teaspoon GROUND CORIANDER

1 tablespoon MIXED CHOPPED NUTS

3 tablespoons REDUCED-CALORIE MAYONNAISE

½ cup FRESHLY GRATED MOZZARELLA CHEESE

SALT AND PEPPER

Wipe and peel the mushrooms. Cook the rice in boiling water for 10 minutes. Drain well. Stir the pineapple, scallions, coriander, nuts and mayonnaise into the rice, and season well. Spoon the rice mixture onto the mushrooms, and top with the mozzarella cheese.

Cook under a medium-hot broiler for 7 minutes, or until the cheese has melted. SERVES 4

Mackerel & Gooseberry Pâté

☙

2 SMOKED MACKEREL FILLETS, SKINNED

¾ cup GOOSEBERRIES, TOPPED AND TAILED

2 teaspoons SUPERFINE SUGAR

1 cup FULL-FAT CREAM CHEESE

2 tablepoons GHERKINS

few drops of TABASCO

grated zest of 1 LIME

2 teaspoons LIME JUICE

To garnish

GREEN OLIVES

DILL SPRIG

Put the mackerel into a bowl, and flake with a fork. Put the gooseberries and sugar into a pan, cover and cook over a low heat for 7 minutes. Let cool.

Put the fish, cheese, gooseberries and gherkins into a food processor, and blend for 30 seconds. Spoon into a bowl, then add the remaining ingredients. Spoon into four individual ramekin dishes. Chill until required. Serve garnished with olives and dill. SERVES 4

TOP: Stuffed Mushrooms

BOTTOM: Mackerel & Gooseberry Pâté

Deep-Fried Brie with Gooseberry Sauce

8 ounces BRIE CHEESE
1 EGG, BEATEN
½ cup WHOLE WHEAT DRIED BREAD CRUMBS
1 tablespoon MIXED CHOPPED NUTS
OIL FOR DEEP-FRYING
1 cup PARSLEY SPRIGS
1 teaspoon SALT

Sauce
1½ cups GOOSEBERRIES, WASHED, TOPPED AND TAILED
3 tablespoons SUPERFINE SUGAR
½ teaspoon GROUND GINGER
2 tablespoons WATER

Cut the Brie cheese into 4 equal-sized pieces. Put the egg into one shallow dish, and the bread crumbs and nuts into another. Dip the cheese into the egg to coat evenly, then into the crumb mixture until completely covered.

Put the gooseberries into a pan with the sugar, ginger and water. Cover and simmer for 15 minutes until soft. Let cool, then strain into a bowl.

Heat the oil to 350°F, and fry the Brie for 3–4 minutes until golden. Remove with a slotted spoon, and drain on paper towels. Add the parsley to the oil, and fry for 1 minute. Remove with a slotted spoon, and drain. Sprinkle with the salt. Place on a serving plate with the Brie, and spoon on the gooseberry sauce. Serve. SERVES 4

Fruit Misto

Batter
1 cup ALL-PURPOSE FLOUR
½ teaspoon SALT
1 tablespoon MELTED BUTTER
⅔ cup WATER
1 EGG WHITE

1 AVOCADO, PEELED, HALVED AND PITTED
1 MANGO, PEELED AND SLICED
8 ounces OGEN MELON, PEELED AND DESEEDED
6 ounces PROSCIUTTO
OIL FOR DEEP-FRYING
LEMON ZEST, TO GARNISH

Lemon Mayonnaise
1 cup REDUCED-CALORIE MAYONNAISE
2 teaspoons LEMON JUICE
1 GARLIC CLOVE, CRUSHED

To make the batter, sift the flour and salt into a bowl. Make a well in the center, then mix to a smooth batter with the butter and water. Beat the egg white until it peaks, then fold into the batter.

Slice the avocado, mango and melon. Heat the oil to 350°F. Coat the fruit in the batter, then fry for 3–4 minutes in the hot oil until golden-brown. Remove with a slotted spoon, and drain on paper towels.

Mix together the ingredients for the lemon mayonnaise, and place in a serving bowl. Arrange the prosciutto and fried fruits on a serving plate. Garnish with lemon zest, and serve with the mayonnaise. SERVES 4

TOP: *Deep-fried Brie with Gooseberry Sauce*
BOTTOM: *Fruit Misto*

Grape & Stilton Puffs

☙

Choux Pastry

²⁄₃ *cup* ALL-PURPOSE FLOUR

pinch of SALT

¼ *cup* BUTTER

²⁄₃ *cup* WATER

2 EGGS, BEATEN

Filling

1 tablespoon BUTTER

2 tablespoons ALL-PURPOSE FLOUR

²⁄₃ *cup* HEAVY CREAM

¹⁄₃ *cup* MILK

1 cup CRUMBLED STILTON CHEESE

½ *cup* GREEN SEEDLESS GRAPES, HALVED

SALT AND PEPPER

GRAPES, TO GARNISH

Preheat the oven to 400°F. Sift the flour for the choux pastry into a bowl with the salt. Melt the butter for the choux pastry in a pan with the water. Bring to a boil, and remove from the heat. Add all the flour to the pan, and beat until the mixture is glossy and comes away from the sides. Let cool slightly, then beat in the eggs gradually until the mixture forms a ball.

Put the mixture into a piping bag, and pipe onto a greased baking sheet. Bake for 20 minutes, or until risen and golden. Remove from the oven, and cut a small slit in the side of each puff. Return to the oven for an additional 5 minutes. Remove and let cool completely.

Melt the butter in a pan, and add the flour. Cook for 1 minute. Stir in the cream, milk and Stilton, then cook for an additional 5 minutes. Stir in the grapes, and season well. Split the choux puffs, and spoon the mixture inside. Serve garnished with grapes.

SERVES 4

Baked Stuffed Mussels

☙

1½ pounds MUSSELS

2½ cups CHICKEN STOCK

1 cup FRESH WHOLE WHEAT BREAD CRUMBS

grated zest and juice of 1 LEMON

grated zest and juice of 1 LIME

1 tablespoon SNIPPED FRESH CHIVES

2 GARLIC CLOVES, CRUSHED

½ RED ONION, FINELY CHOPPED

2 tablespoons MAYONNAISE

Dip

1¼ cups SOUR CREAM

2 GARLIC CLOVES, CRUSHED

grated zest of 1 LIME

1 tablespoon CHOPPED FRESH DILL

Scrub the mussels under running water to remove the "beards" and barnacles. Discard any open mussels. Cook the mussels in the stock for 5–7 minutes. Drain the mussels, discarding the stock and any mussels that are closed. Break the empty half of the shell from each mussel, and discard.

Mix together the crumbs, lemon and lime zest and juices, chives, garlic, onion and mayonnaise. Spoon onto the cooked mussels, and cook under a medium-hot broiler for 3–4 minutes.

Meanwhile, mix together the dip ingredients. Serve with the hot mussels.

SERVES 4

TOP: Grape & Stilton Puffs
BOTTOM: Baked Stuffed Mussels

Salads

The addition of fruits to salads opens the door to a feast of flavors, adding color and variety to these light meals and accompaniments. Their fresh, sweet flavors combine perfectly with savory ingredients to provide an array of delicious salads.

Bean Medley

❦

½ *cup* RED KIDNEY BEANS
½ *cup* GARBANZO BEANS
½ *cup* BLACK-EYED PEAS
1 RED ONION
¼ *cup* CHOPPED SHELLED BRAZIL NUTS
½ *cup* QUARTERED SEEDLESS GREEN GRAPES
2 *teaspoons* CHOPPED FRESH CILANTRO, TO GARNISH

Dressing
3 *tablespoons* OLIVE OIL
4 *teaspoons* GARLIC WINE VINEGAR
1 *teaspoons* PREPARED MUSTARD
pinch of SUGAR

Soak the kidney beans, garbanzo beans and black-eyed peas in water overnight. Drain and put into a pan. Cover with clean water, and bring to a boil. Boil rapidly for 10 minutes, then drain. Return to the pan, and cover with water. Simer for 1 hour, or until thoroughly cooked. Drain and let cool.

Put the beans into a serving bowl. Halve and slice the red onion, then add to the beans with the nuts and grapes.

Put all the dressing ingredients into a screw-top jar, and shake well. Pour over the beans, and serve, garnished with cilantro.   SERVES 4

Smoked Turkey & Raspberry Salad

❦

1 *pound* COOKED SMOKED TURKEY
¾ *cup* RASPBERRIES, WASHED
3 *tablespoons* RASPBERRY VINEGAR
5 *tablespoons* OLIVE OIL
½ *teaspoon* PREPARED MUSTARD
1½ *cups* SALAD GREENS
6 SCALLIONS, TRIMMED AND HALVED

Cut the turkey into slices. Put the raspberries, vinegar, oil and mustard into a pan, and heat gently for 2–3 minutes. Arrange the turkey, salad greens and scallions in a bowl. Pour the hot raspberry dressing over, and serve immediately.   SERVES 4

TOP: Bean Medley
BOTTOM: Smoked Turkey & Raspberry Salad

Sole & Shrimp Salad

☙

1½ *pounds* SOLE FILLET
2 *cups* SHELLED SMALL SHRIMP
1 MANGO, PEELED
¼ *cup* GHERKINS, HALVED LENGTHWISE
2 *tablespoons* GREEN STUFFED OLIVES, HALVED
2-inch piece CUCUMBER, CUT INTO STRIPS
1 *tablespoon* CHOPPED FRESH DILL
1 *cup* RADICCHIO
2 *teaspoons* SESAME SEEDS

Dressing
4 *tablespoons* SESAME OIL
2 *tablespoons* LEMON JUICE
pinch of SUGAR

Put the sole into a pan, cover with water, and poach for 7 minutes. Remove from the pan, and skin. Let cool, then cut the flesh into strips. Put the fish into a bowl with the shrimp.

Dice the mango flesh, and add to the bowl with the gherkins, olives, cucumber and dill. Arrange the radicchio in a bowl, and spoon on the fish mixture. Sprinkle on the sesame seeds.

Put all the dressing ingredients into a screw-top jar, and shake well. Pour over the salad, and serve.　SERVES 4

Sunrise Salad

☙

1 GRAPEFRUIT
1 LARGE ORANGE
½ HONEYDEW MELON
1 CHARENTAIS MELON
¼ WHITE CABBAGE, SHREDDED
1 RED BELL PEPPER, SEEDED AND DICED
1 *tablespoon* CLEAR HONEY
2 *tablespoons* OLIVE OIL
SALT AND PEPPER

Peel and cut the grapefruit and orange into segments, removing all the pith and reserving any juice. Seed and peel the melons, and cut into slices. Arrange all the fruits and vegetables on a plate in strips of color.

Mix together the reserved fruit juices, honey and oil. Season, and pour over the salad. Serve.　SERVES 4

TOP: Sole & Shrimp Salad
BOTTOM: Sunrise Salad

Goat Cheese & Melon Salad

☙

8 SLICES WHITE BREAD
¼ *cup* BUTTER
2 GARLIC CLOVES, CRUSHED
1 *pound* GOAT CHEESE
1 *pound* WATERMELON
1 *tablespoon* CHOPPED FRESH PARSLEY, TO GARNISH

To Serve
RADICCHIO
CORN SALAD

Dressing
½ *teaspoon* WHOLE GRAIN MUSTARD
4 *tablespoons* OLIVE OIL
2 *tablespoons* GARLIC VINEGAR

Cut out eight 5-inch rounds from the bread. Melt the butter in a pan. Add the garlic and the bread rounds, and fry, turning, for 2–3 minutes, until golden. Remove and keep warm. Slice the goat cheese into eight equal pieces. Peel and deseed the watermelon, then cut the flesh into cubes.

Put all the dressing ingredients into a screw-top jar, and shake well. Arrange the salad greens on a plate with the watermelon. Place a piece of cheese on top of each bread croûte, then place on top of the salad. Pour the dressing over, and serve. SERVES 4

Spinach & Peach Salad

☙

8 *ounces* SPINACH, TRIMMED
12 *ounces* FETA CHEESE
1 YELLOW BELL PEPPER, SEEDED AND SLICED
2 PEACHES
1 AVOCADO, PEELED

Dressing
2 *tablespoons* OLIVE OIL
1 GARLIC CLOVE, CRUSHED
1 *tablespoon* CIDER VINEGAR
2 *teaspoons* CHOPPED FRESH OREGANO
2 *teaspoons* LEMON JUICE

Rinse the spinach, and pat dry. Put into a serving bowl. Cut the cheese into dice, and add to the bowl with the bell pepper. Halve the peaches, remove the pits and slice the flesh. Halve the avocado, remove the pit and slice. Add to the bowl with the peaches.

Put all the dressing ingredients into a screw-top jar, and shake well. Pour over the salad, and serve. SERVES 4

Top: Goat Cheese & Melon Salad
Bottom: Spinach & Peach Salad

Fruity Bulgar Salad

🍎

2 cups BULGAR WHEAT
3 GARLIC CLOVES, CRUSHED
1 RED ONION, HALVED AND SLICED
4 ounces APRICOTS
2 tablespoons CHOPPED FRESH CILANTRO
3 RADISHES, WASHED, TRIMMED AND SLICED
2 tablespoons PINE NUTS
SALT AND PEPPER

Dressing
3 tablespoons OLIVE OIL
4 teaspoons GARLIC WINE VINEGAR
1 GARLIC CLOVE, CRUSHED
½ teaspoon PREPARED MUSTARD

Put the bulgar wheat into a bowl, and pour on enough boiling water to cover. Let sit for 10–15 minutes. Drain off any liquid, if necessary. Add the garlic and onion to the bulgar wheat. Halve the apricots, and remove the pits. Slice the fruit, and add to the bulgar wheat with the cilantro, radishes and pine nuts. Season and mix well.

Put the dressing ingredients into a screw-top jar, and shake well. Pour over the salad, and serve.   SERVES 4

Fruity Chicken Salad

🍎

3 cups DICED COOKED CHICKEN
1 MANGO, PEELED
1 BANANA
1 teaspoon LEMON JUICE
⅔ cup SOUR CREAM
4 tablespoons REDUCED-CALORIE MAYONNAISE
2 tablespoons MANGO CHUTNEY
2 teaspoons CURRY PASTE
6 FRESH FIGS, WASHED AND QUARTERED
1 tablespoon SLIVERED ALMONDS

Put the chicken into a bowl. Cut the flesh from the mango, and add to the chicken. Chop the banana, and toss in the lemon juice. Add to the chicken and mango. Mix together the sour cream, mayonnaise, mango chutney and curry paste. Spoon over the chicken, and mix together well.

Arrange the quartered figs around the outside of the serving plate. Spoon the chicken mixture into the center. Sprinkle on the almonds, and serve.   SERVES 4

TOP: Fruity Bulgar Salad
BOTTOM: Fruit Chicken Salad

Vegetarian Meals

Fruits are a perfect complement to the traditional blandness of vegetarian food, by adding color and texture to the dishes. The recipes in this chapter have a distinctly cosmopolitan quality, and will be equally tempting to those who are not vegetarians.

Stuffed Eggplants

☙

2 EGGPLANTS, WASHED
½ cup BULGAR WHEAT
6 ounces APRICOTS, WASHED
⅓ cup DATES, WASHED, PITTED AND CHOPPED
¼ cup CHOPPED HAZELNUTS
1 tablespoon CHOPPED FRESH CILANTRO
½ cup GRATED VEGETARIAN HARD CHEESE
SALT AND PEPPER

Halve the eggplants lengthwise. Scoop out the center with a teaspoon, and put the scooped flesh into a bowl. Put the bulgar wheat into a separate bowl, and cover with boiling water. Let sit for 10–15 minutes, then drain if necessary. Add the eggplant flesh to the bulgar wheat.

Halve the apricots; remove the pits, and chop the flesh. Add to the bulgar wheat mixture with the dates, hazelnuts and cilantro. Season well. Spoon into the hollowed-out eggplants, and top with the cheese. Cook under a medium-hot broiler for 7–10 minutes. SERVES 4

Vegetable Tortillas

☙

4 WHEAT TORTILLAS

Filling
1 tablespoon OLIVE OIL
1 ONION, CHOPPED
1 RED BELL PEPPER, SEEDED AND CHOPPED
⅔ cup LONG-GRAIN AND WILD RICE
1 teaspoon CHILI POWDER
⅓ cup DRAINED CANNED RED KIDNEY BEANS
1¼ cups VEGETABLE STOCK
1¾ cups PEELED, CORED AND CHOPPED
FRESH PINEAPPLE
SOUR CREAM
SALSA

To make the filling, heat the oil, then add the onion and bell pepper, and fry for 3 minutes. Stir in the rice and chili powder. Add the beans, stock and pineapple, and cook for 20 minutes. Put the tortillas into the mixture briefly to soften. Remove and spoon in the filling. Roll up, and serve with sour cream and salsa. SERVES 4

TOP: Stuffed Eggplants
BOTTOM: Vegetable Tortillas

Spanakopita

☙

6 ounces	FILO PASTRY
2 tablespoons	MELTED BUTTER
3½ cups	SPINACH, WASHED AND TRIMMED
1 cup	COTTAGE CHEESE
1½ cups	FRESH PINEAPPLE, PEELED, CORED AND DICED
⅓ cup	DRAINED, CANNED GARBANZO BEANS
½ teaspoon	GROUND NUTMEG
2	EGGS, BEATEN
	SALT AND PEPPER

Cover the base and sides of an ovenproof dish with 3 sheets of filo pastry, then brush with melted butter. Repeat twice more. Blanch the spinach in boiling water for 2 minutes, then drain well. Place in the bottom of the dish.

Preheat the oven to 375°F. Mix together the cheese, pineapple and garbanzo beans. Season and add the nutmeg. Stir in the eggs. Spoon the mixture over the spinach in the lined dish. Lay 2 further sheets of filo pastry on top, then brush them with melted butter. Layer the remaining filo pastry on top, brushing with butter. Pour any remaining melted butter over, and bake for 40 minutes. Serve with salad. SERVES 4

Stir-Fried Vegetables

☙

1 tablespoon	OLIVE OIL
4 ounces	BROCCOLI, CUT INTO FLOWERETS
2 ounces	SNOW PEAS
1	YELLOW ZUCCHINI, CUT INTO JULIENNE STRIPS
1	CARROT, CUT INTO JULIENNE STRIPS
1	RED BELL PEPPER, SEEDED AND DICED
⅓ cup	DRAINED, CANNED BAMBOO SHOOTS
½-inch piece	GINGERROOT, PEELED AND CHOPPED
1 teaspoon	CHINESE FIVE-SPICE POWDER
8	LYCHEES, PEELED AND QUARTERED
2	KUMQUATS, SLICED
2 tablespoons	LIGHT SOY SAUCE
2 tablespoons	ORANGE MARMALADE

Heat the oil in a wok or large skillet until almost smoking. Add the broccoli, snow peas, zucchini, carrot and bell pepper. Stir-fry for 5 minutes. Add the bamboo shoots, gingerroot, five-spice powder, lychees and kumquats. Stir in the soy sauce and marmalade, then cook for an additional 7 minutes, stirring. Serve with freshly cooked noodles. SERVES 4

TOP: Spanakopita
BOTTOM: Stir-Fried Vegetables

Rissoles

꩜

1 pound POTATOES, DICED
1 CARROT, DICED
3 SCALLIONS, DICED
1 CELERY STALK, DICED
1 EGG, BEATEN
2 cups FRESH WHOLE WHEAT BREAD CRUMBS
OIL FOR DEEP-FRYING

Sauce
1 tablespoon SESAME OIL
2 PEACHES, PITTED AND CHOPPED
2 tablespoons CLEAR HONEY
1 tablespoon ALL-PURPOSE FLOUR
⅔ cup VEGETABLE STOCK

Boil the potatoes in salted water for 20 minutes. Drain well, and mash. Transfer to a bowl, and let cool slightly. Add the vegetables, then stir together to form a firm mixture. Roll into 8 sausage shapes. Dip the rissoles into the beaten egg to coat evenly, and then into the bread crumbs to cover. Heat the oil for deep-frying to 350°F. Fry the rissoles for 3–5 minutes, or until golden. Remove with a slotted spoon, and drain on paper towels; keep warm.

Heat the sesame oil in a pan. Add the peaches and honey, and cook for 5 minutes. Add the flour and stock, then bring to a boil. Season and cook the sauce for an additional 5 minutes. SERVES 4

Samosas

꩜

2 tablespoons BUTTER
2 CELERY STALKS, CHOPPED
3 tablespoons FROZEN PEAS
1 POTATO, DICED
¼ cup GROUND CHERRIES
1 MANGO, PEELED AND DICED
1 teaspoon GARAM MASALA
½ teaspoon GROUND CUMIN
8 ounces FILO PASTRY
2 tablespoons MELTED BUTTER
OIL FOR DEEP-FRYING

Melt the butter in a pan. Add the vegetables and fruit. Stir in the garam masala and cumin, then cook for 10 minutes. Cut the filo pastry sheets in half, and divide into 8 equal piles. Brush each sheet with melted butter, and form into piles again. Spoon the filling into one corner of the top sheet of each pile. Brush the edges of the pastry with the melted butter, then fold into triangles.

Heat the oil to 350°F, and fry the samosas for 3–5 minutes, or until golden-brown. Drain well, and serve with Indian pickle. SERVES 4

TOP: Rissoles

BOTTOM: Samosas

Vegetable Crêpes

❦

Crêpes
1 cup ALL-PURPOSE FLOUR
1 EGG, BEATEN
1¼ cups MILK
grated zest of 1 ORANGE

Filling
1 tablespoon BUTTER
2 tablespoons ALL-PURPOSE FLOUR
⅔ cup VEGETABLE STOCK
⅔ cup MILK
½ cup GRATED PARMESAN CHEESE
2 tablespoons DRAINED, CANNED CORN
¼ cup FROZEN GREEN BEANS
½ cup CAULIFLOWER FLOWERETS
1 RED EATING APPLE, CORED AND SLICED
¼ cup REDCURRANTS
SALT AND PEPPER

Sift the flour for the crêpes with a pinch of salt into a bowl. Make a well in the center, and add the egg. Beat in the milk and orange zest to form a smooth batter.

Melt the butter for the filling in a pan, then add the flour, and cook for 1 minute. Remove from the heat, and stir in the stock, milk and cheese. Return to the heat, and bring to a boil, stirring. Season well. Stir in the vegetables and apple, and cook for an additional 10 minutes. Add the redcurrants, and cook for an additional 5 minutes.

Meanwhile, pour one-eighth of the batter into a non-stick heated pancake pan. Cook for 2–3 minutes on each side, remove and keep warm. Repeat with the remaining batter.

Spoon the vegetable mixture into the crêpes. Fold the crêpes over, roll up and serve.   SERVES 4

Goat Cheese & Grape Tart

❦

10 ounces PREPARED PLAIN PASTRY DOUGH

Filling
1 pound GOAT CHEESE
2 EGGS, BEATEN
2 tablespoons CHOPPED FRESH TARRAGON
1 teaspoon PREPARED MUSTARD
½ cup QUARTERED SEEDLESS GREEN GRAPES
BEATEN EGG, TO GLAZE

Preheat the oven to 375°F. Roll out enough of the pastry dough to line an 8-inch fluted pie pan. Bake the pie shell for 15 minutes. Mix together the goat cheese, eggs, tarragon, mustard and grapes. Spoon the mixture into the pie shell.

Roll out the remaining pastry dough and cut into strips. Arrange on top of the tart in a lattice pattern, and brush with egg. Bake for 25 minutes.   SERVES 6

TOP: Vegetable Crêpes
BOTTOM: Goat Cheese & Grape Tart

Vegetable Wellington

☙

1½ *cups* BULGAR WHEAT

⅔ *cup* VEGETABLE STOCK

2 *tablespoons* CHOPPED FRESH CILANTRO

1 POMEGRANATE, HALVED

1 MANDARIN, PEELED AND SEGMENTED

1⅓ *cups* SLICED OPEN CAP MUSHROOMS

2 TOMATOES, SLICED

1 *pound* PREPARED PUFF PASTRY

1 EGG, BEATEN, TO GLAZE

SALT AND PEPPER

Put the bulgar wheat in a pan with the stock. Bring to a boil, and simmer for 15 minutes. Stir in the cilantro. Scoop out the pomegranate flesh, then add to the bulgar wheat and season. Stir in the mandarin segments, and let cool.

Preheat the oven to 400°F. Roll out the pastry dough to a 12 × 14-inch rectangle. Spoon the bulgar wheat filling along the center of the dough. Top with the mushrooms and tomatoes. Brush the edges of the dough with beaten egg, and fold around the filling to encase completely. Place on a dampened baking sheet, seam-side down. Brush with the remaining egg, and garnish with any dough trimmings. Bake for 40 minutes, or until risen and golden.

SERVES 8

Risotto

☙

2 *tablespoons* OLIVE OIL

1⅓ *cups* ARBORIO RICE

1 ONION, CHOPPED

1 CARROT, GRATED

1 ZUCCHINI, DICED

4 BABY CORN, HALVED LENGTHWISE

⅔ *cup* SLICED CRIMINI MUSHROOMS

2 *cups* SKINNED AND DICED COD FILLET

⅔ *cup* GOOSEBERRIES, TOPPED AND TAILED

2½ *cups* VEGETABLE STOCK

SALT AND PEPPER

2 *tablespoons* CHOPPED FRESH PARSLEY, TO GARNISH

Heat the oil in a pan. Add the rice, and fry for 2 minutes. Stir in the onion, carrot, zucchini and corn. Fry for an additional 5 minutes.

Add the mushrooms, fish, gooseberries and stock. Season, then simmer over a low heat for 25 minutes. Sprinkle with parsley, and serve.

SERVES 4

TOP: *Vegetable Wellington*

BOTTOM: *Risotto*

Main Meals

Not confined to sweet dishes, fruits play an important role in many excellent entrées. Combining well with savory ingredients, they are used extensively in sauces and stuffings, as well as being a principal ingredient in poultry, meat and fish dishes.

Duck with Red Cabbage & Orange

☙

3¼-pound OVEN-READY DUCK
1 ONION, HALVED
½ RED CABBAGE
2 ORANGES, PEELED AND CUT INTO SEGMENTS
⅔ cup ORANGE JUICE
⅔ cup CHICKEN STOCK
3 tablespoons CHOPPED PITTED DATES
1½ tablespoons CORNSTARCH
3 tablespoons WATER

Heat the oven to 400°F. Wash the duck inside and out, then prick the skin with a fork. Place the onion inside the cavity.

Shred the red cabbage, and put in the bottom of a flameproof casserole. Add the orange segments, juice and stock. Stir in the dates, and place the duck on top. Cover the casserole, and bake for 1 hour. Remove the lid and cook for an additional 10 minutes.

Remove the duck from the casserole, and keep warm. Blend the cornstarch with the water, and stir into the cabbage mixture. Bring to a boil on the stove top, and cook until thickened.

Shred the duck, then spoon the red cabbage and orange mixture onto a serving plate. Top with the shredded duck and serve.   SERVES 4

RIGHT: Duck with Red Cabbage & Orange

Chicken Curry

🍎

1 tablespoon OLIVE OIL

1 ONION, CHOPPED

2 GARLIC CLOVES, CRUSHED

1 teaspoon CURRY PASTE

1 teaspoon GARAM MASALA

1 teaspoon GROUND CUMIN

1 teaspoon GROUND CORIANDER

1 pound BONELESS CHICKEN BREAST HALVES, SKINNED

1¼ cups CHICKEN STOCK

2 tablespoons GROUND ALMONDS

1 MANGO, PEELED

1 BANANA, SLICED

⅔ cup NATURAL YOGURT

SALT AND PEPPER

CHOPPED FRESH CILANTRO, TO GARNISH

Heat the oil in a pan. Add the onion, garlic, curry paste, garam masala, cumin and ground coriander. Fry for 5 minutes, stirring. Add the chicken breast halves, and fry for 5 minutes. Stir in the stock, then bring to a boil. Stir in the ground almonds, reduce the heat, and simmer for 20 minutes.

Dice the mango flesh, and add to the curry with the banana and yogurt. Season and simmer for an additional 5 minutes. Serve with rice. SERVES 4

Pork with Cider & Plums

🍎

2 pounds PORK TENDERLOIN

1 tablespoon BUTTER

1 tablespoon OLIVE OIL

1 tablespoon ALL-PURPOSE FLOUR

⅔ cup VEGETABLE STOCK

⅔ cup HEAVY CREAM

⅔ cup DRY CIDER

1 PEAR, PEELED, CORED AND SLICED

2 cups PITTED AND SLICED PLUMS

Slice the pork tenderloin, and trim off any excess fat. Heat the butter and oil in a skillet, then add the pork and fry for 10 minutes, stirring constantly. Add the flour, and cook for 1 minute longer. Stir in the stock, cream and cider, then bring to a boil. Reduce the heat, and simmer for 15 minutes. Stir in the pear and plums, then simmer for an additional 5 minutes. SERVES 4

TOP: Pork with Cider & Plums
BOTTOM: Chicken Curry

Lamb Couscous

☙

1 tablespoon OLIVE OIL
3 cups CUBED LAMB
1 ONION, QUARTERED
1 CARROT, DICED
1 ZUCCHINI, CUT INTO CHUNKS
2 BABY TURNIPS, DICED
¼ cup ALL-PURPOSE FLOUR
2 cups LAMB STOCK
4 ounces FRESH APRICOTS
1 tablespoon CHOPPED FRESH CILANTRO
1 tablespoon CLEAR HONEY
1½ cups BULGAR WHEAT
⅔ cup WATER

Heat the oil in a pan. Add the lamb, and fry for 5 minutes, stirring constantly. Add the onion, carrot, zucchini and turnips, and cook for an additional 5 minutes. Add the flour, and cook for 1 minute. Stir in the stock, reduce the heat, cover and cook for 40 minutes. Halve and pit the apricots, and cut the flesh into quarters. Add to the pan with the cilantro and honey. Cover and simmer for an additional 10 minutes.

Meanwhile, put the bulgar wheat into a separate pan with the water. Bring to a boil, reduce the heat, and simmer for 10 minutes, or until cooked. Spoon onto a serving plate, and top with the lamb mixture. Serve.

SERVES 4

Lamb Noisettes

☙

1 tablespoon OLIVE OIL
1 tablespoon BUTTER
4 LAMB NOISETTES
2 GARLIC CLOVES, CRUSHED
⅔ cup CRANBERRY JUICE
⅔ cup LAMB STOCK
½ cup FRESH CRANBERRIES, WASHED
1 tablespoon CHOPPED FRESH ROSEMARY
4 teaspoons CORNSTARCH
3 tablespoons WATER
SALT AND PEPPER

Croûtes
2 tablespoons BUTTER
4 SLICES WHITE BREAD

Heat the oil and butter in a skillet. Add the lamb and garlic, then cook for 10 minutes, turning frequently. Stir in the cranberry juice and stock, then add the cranberries and rosemary. Blend the cornstarch with the water. Stir into the lamb mixture, and bring to a boil. Season and cook for 10 minutes.

Meanwhile, melt the butter for the croûtes in a separate skillet. Stamp out four 4-inch rounds of bread, and fry in the butter, turning frequently, for 5 minutes, until golden. Remove the noisettes from the skillet, and place one on each croûte. Place on a serving plate, and spoon the sauce around. Serve with freshly cooked vegetables.

SERVES 4

TOP: Lamb Couscous
BOTTOM: Lamb Noisettes

Baked Ham & Bananas

❦

3¼-pound HAM
20 CLOVES
3 tablespoons LIME MARMALADE
¼ cup SOFT DARK BROWN SUGAR
4 BANANAS, PEELED
¼ cup SOFT LIGHT BROWN SUGAR
grated zest and juice of 2 LIMES

Put the ham into a pan of water. Bring to a boil, and cook for 1 hour. Take out of the pan, and remove the skin and fat. Score the top of the ham to form a diamond pattern. Stud the top of the ham with cloves.

Preheat the oven to 375°F. Put the marmalade and sugar into a pan over a low heat until melted, then spoon on top of the ham. Place the ham on a trivet in a baking pan, and bake for 1 hour 20 minutes.

Put the bananas into a separate roasting pan. Add the sugar, lime juice and zest. Bake one shelf above the ham for the last 10 minutes of cooking time. Serve. SERVES 4

Turkey Roll

❦

4 SKINNED TURKEY ESCALOPES
2 cups FRESH WHITE BREAD CRUMBS
½ cup RASPBERRIES, WASHED
1 tablespoon SNIPPED FRESH CHIVES
1 tablespoon MIXED CHOPPED NUTS
1 EGG, BEATEN
6 slices RINDLESS BACON
2 tablespoons CRANBERRY SAUCE
SALT AND PEPPER

Preheat the oven to 375°F. Place the turkey escalopes between two sheets of plastic wrap. Beat with a meat mallet to ¼-inch thickness, or until the escalopes are joined together. Mix together the bread crumbs, raspberries, chives and nuts. Season and add the beaten egg.

Spread the mixture evenly on top of the turkey, and roll up. Wrap the bacon slices around the turkey roll. Heat the cranberry sauce in a pan until melted, and brush onto the bacon. Bake the roll for 1 hour. Serve with freshly cooked vegetables. SERVES 4

TOP: *Baked Ham & Bananas*
BOTTOM: *Turkey Roll*

Baked Stuffed Trout

☙

4 RAINBOW TROUT

2 *cups* FRESH WHOLE WHEAT BREAD CRUMBS

1 ORANGE, PEELED, CUT INTO SEGMENTS AND CHOPPED

1 GRAPEFRUIT, PEELED, CUT INTO SEGMENTS AND CHOPPED

2 *tablespoons* CHOPPED FRESH PARSLEY

1 CELERY STALK, SLICED

1 GARLIC CLOVE, CRUSHED

1 EGG, BEATEN

Preheat the oven to 400°F. Clean and gut the fish. Remove the fins.

Mix together the bread crumbs, orange, grapefruit, parsley, celery and garlic. Stir in the egg, and mix together. Place the stuffing mixture inside the prepared fish. Wrap the fish in buttered foil, and bake for 25 minutes. Serve with salad. SERVES 4

Fruity Ham Fry

☙

1 *tablespoon* OLIVE OIL

3 *cups* CUBED, COOKED HAM

2 *ounces* SNOW PEAS

⅔ *cup* FRESH PINEAPPLE, PEELED, CORED AND CUBED

1 RUBY GRAPEFRUIT, PEELED AND CUT INTO SEGMENTS

2 *cups* BEAN SPROUTS

1 RED BELL PEPPER, SEEDED AND SLICED

2 *tablespoons* SOY SAUCE

1 *tablespoon* CLEAR HONEY

1 *piece* STAR ANISE

1 *teaspoon* CHINESE FIVE-SPICE POWDER

Heat the oil in a wok or large skillet until almost smoking. Add the ham, and stir-fry for 5 minutes. Add the snow peas, pineapple, grapefruit, bean sprouts and bell pepper, then cook for an additional 5 minutes. Stir in the soy sauce, honey, star anise and five-spice powder. Stir-fry for an additional 5 minutes. Remove the star anise, and serve with freshly cooked noodles. SERVES 4

TOP: *Baked Stuffed Trout*
BOTTOM: *Fruity Ham Fry*

Citus Chicken

⚘

¼ *cup* BUTTER

4 BONELESS CHICKEN BREAST HALVES, SKINNED

grated zest and juice of 2 ORANGES

1 ORANGE, PEELED AND CUT INTO SEGMENTS

3 *tablespoons* CLEAR HONEY

⅔ *cup* VEGETABLE STOCK

WATERCRESS, TO GARNISH

Melt the butter in a pan, and fry the chicken for 10 minutes, turning frequently, until browned. Add the orange zest, juice and segments, honey and stock. Cook for 20 minutes, or until the juices run clear when each piece is pierced with the tip of a knife. Garnish with watercress, and serve with freshly cooked rice. SERVES 4

Seafood Gumbo

⚘

2 *tablespoons* BUTTER

1 ONION, CHOPPED

¼ *cup* ALL-PURPOSE FLOUR

5 *cups* FISH STOCK

1½ *cups* SHELLED TIGER SHRIMPS

1½ *cups* WHITE CRABMEAT

8 *ounces* SCALLOPS

TABASCO, TO TASTE

2 CHORIZO SAUSAGES, SLICED

1 *tablespoon* CHOPPED FRESH DILL

grated zest and juice of 1 LIME

8 *ounces* MUSSELS, SCRUBBED

1⅓ *cups* LONG-GRAIN WHITE RICE

Melt the butter in a pan. Add the onion, and sauté for 5 minutes. Then stir in the flour, and cook for 1 minute. Remove from the heat, and stir in the stock. Return to the heat, and bring to a boil; boil for 3 minutes. Add the shrimps, crab, scallops, Tabasco, sausage, dill, lime juice and zest. Cook over a medium heat for 5 minutes. Add the prepared mussels, and cook for an additional 5 minutes.

Meanwhile, boil the rice in a separate pan for 10–12 minutes, then spoon into a serving bowl. Top with the seafood gumbo, and serve. SERVES 4

TOP: Citrus Chicken
BOTTOM: Seafood Gumbo

Quick Meals & Snacks

Quick meals are something most of us require on a constantly expanding scale. The recipes in this chapter give a colorful and flavorsome slant to traditional snacks, combining unusual flavors in kebabs, enchiladas, pizzas and burgers.

Chicken Kebabs

2½ *cups* SKINNED AND DICED CHICKEN BREAST
½ *cup* RED SEEDLESS GRAPES
12 LYCHEES, PEELED
12 GROUND CHERRIES, PEELED
1 GREEN BELL PEPPER, SEEDED AND DICED
8 CHERRY TOMATOES

Marinade
1 *tablespoon* OLIVE OIL
1 *tablespoon* CLEAR HONEY
1 *teaspoon* LEMON JUICE
1 GARLIC CLOVE, CRUSHED
1 *tablespoon* CHOPPED FRESH PARSLEY

Put the chicken into a shallow dish with the grapes, lychees, ground cherries, bell pepper and tomatoes. Mix the marinade ingredients together, and pour over. Cover and chill for 1 hour.

Thread the chicken and fruit onto skewers, and cook, turning once, under a medium-hot broiler for 10–15 minutes, or until the juices run clear when each piece of chicken is pierced with the tip of a knife. Serve with salad.

SERVES 4

Corned Beef Hash

8 *ounces* POTATOES, CUBED
1 *tablespoon* BUTTER
1 *tablespoon* OLIVE OIL
1 ONION, CHOPPED
1 GREEN BELL PEPPER, SEEDED AND DICED
1¼ *cups* CHOPPED, CANNED PRESSED BEEF
1 POMEGRANATE, HALVED
½ *cup* CORED, PEELED AND CUBED
FRESH PINEAPPLE
SALT AND PEPPER

Cook the potatoes in boiling salted water for 10 minutes, or until soft. Drain well and reserve. Heat the butter and oil in a skillet, and add the potato. Fry for 2–3 minutes, stirring constantly. Add the onion and bell pepper, and fry for an additional 2 minutes. Stir in the chopped beef and pineapple, and scoop the pomegranate seeds into the mixture. Season and cook for 2–3 minutes, stirring constantly. Serve.

SERVES 4

TOP: *Chicken Kebabs*
BOTTOM: *Corned Beef Hash*

Citrus Burgers

🍎

½ *cup* BULGAR WHEAT
1⅓ *cups* LEAN GROUND BEEF
1 ONION, CHOPPED
1 GARLIC CLOVE, CHOPPED
¼ *cup* MIXED CHOPPED NUTS
1 ORANGE, PEELED AND CUT INTO SEGMENTS
1 *tablespoon* FRESHLY GRATED PARMESAN CHEESE
1 *tablespoon* SNIPPED FRESH CHIVES
1 EGG, BEATEN
4 SESAME BURGER BUNS
SALAD GREENS
TOMATO RELISH

Put the bulgar wheat into a bowl, and cover with boiling water. Let sit for 10–15 minutes, then drain if necessary. Put the ground beef into a bowl, then add the bulgar wheat, onion, garlic and nuts. Chop the orange segments, and add to the beef mixture. Stir in the Parmesan, chives and egg, and mix together to form a firm mixture.

Divide the mixture into four equal parts. Shape into burgers on a lightly floured counter. Cook, turning once, under a medium-hot broiler for 8–10 minutes, or until cooked through. Place in a split burger bun with the salad greens and tomato relish, and serve.   SERVES 4

Stuffed Pineapple

🍎

2 *baby* PINEAPPLES

Filling
1 *tablespoon* OLIVE OIL
1 ONION, CHOPPED
1 *cup* LEAN GROUND BEEF
1 *teaspoon* GROUND CUMIN
1 *teaspoon* GROUND CORIANDER
1 *tablespoon* ALL-PURPOSE FLOUR
⅔ *cup* BEEF STOCK
1 *tablespoon* WORCESTERSHIRE SAUCE
1 *tablespoon* CHOPPED FRESH PARSLEY
¼ *cup* GRATED CHEDDAR CHEESE

Halve the pineapples lengthwise, and remove the cores. Scoop out the flesh, leaving a ½-inch rim.

To make the filling, heat the oil in a pan, and fry the onion and beef for 5 minutes. Add the cumin and coriander, and fry for an additional 2 minutes. Stir in the flour, and cook for 1 minute. Add the stock, Worcestershire sauce and parsley, then simmer for 20 minutes.

Stir in the reserved pineapple flesh, then spoon the mixture into the pineapple cases. Top with the cheese, and cook under a medium-hot broiler for 7 minutes, or until the cheese has melted.   SERVES 4

TOP: Citrus Burgers
BOTTOM: Stuffed Pineapple

Smoky Pasta

❧

1 tablespoon OLIVE OIL
1 ONION, CHOPPED
2 GARLIC CLOVES, CRUSHED
1 tablespoon ALL-PURPOSE FLOUR
⅔ cup HEAVY CREAM
⅓ cup DRY WHITE WINE
¾ cup DICED SMOKED MEAT
3 FIGS, WASHED AND CHOPPED
2 tablespoons CHOPPED FRESH BASIL
2 cups PENNE

Heat the oil in a pan. Add the onion and garlic, and fry for 5 minutes. Stir in the flour, and cook for 1 minute longer. Add the cream and wine, then bring to a boil, stirring constantly. Add the smoked meat and basil, then cook over a medium heat for 5 minutes. Stir in the figs, and cook for an additional 2–3 minutes.

Meanwhile, cook the pasta in boiling salted water for 8–10 minutes, or until *al dente*. Drain well, and spoon into warmed serving dishes. Spoon the pasta sauce on top, and serve immediately.

SERVES 4

Fruity Pizza

❧

Dough
4 cups SELF-RISING FLOUR
½ cup BUTTER
1 cup MILK

Topping
1¼ cups CHOPPED COOKED CHICKEN
1 GREEN BELL PEPPER, SEEDED AND SLICED
¼ cup CANNED CORN, DRAINED
¾ cup PEELED, CORED AND DICED FRESH PINEAPPLE
1 BANANA, DICED
2 ounces MOZZARELLA CHEESE, SLICED

Sauce
1 tablespoon BUTTER
2 tablespoons ALL-PURPOSE FLOUR
1 cup MILK
¼ cup FRESHLY GRATED CHEDDAR CHEESE
1 tablespoon CHOPPED FRESH TARRAGON
SALT AND PEPPER

To make the dough, sift the flour and a pinch of salt into a bowl. Rub in the butter until the mixture resembles bread crumbs. Make a well in the center, then add the milk and bring together to form a smooth dough. Roll out into an 8-inch round on a lightly floured counter. Place on a greased baking sheet.

Preheat the oven to 400°F. Melt the butter for the sauce, then add the flour and cook for 1 minute. Stir in the milk, cheese and tarragon. Season and bring to a boil, stirring constantly. Spoon onto the pizza base. Top with the remaining ingredients, and bake for 30 minutes, or until the cheese has melted. Serve with a green salad.

SERVES 4

TOP: Smoky Pasta
BOTTOM: Fruity Pizza

Twice-Baked Potatoes

🍅

4 LARGE BAKING POTATOES

SALT

1 tablespoon OLIVE OIL

Filling

¾ *cup* CHOPPED COOKED CHICKEN

⅔ *cup* NATURAL YOGURT

1 BANANA, SLICED

1 PEACH, HALVED, PITTED AND CHOPPED

1 tablespoon SNIPPED FRESH CHIVES

¼ *cup* GRATED COLBY CHEESE

Preheat the oven to 400°F. Prick the potatoes, and place in a roasting pan. Sprinkle the salt over, and pour the oil over. Bake for 1 hour, or until cooked through.

Remove the potatoes from the oven, and cut in half lengthwise. Scoop out the centers, and put the potato into a bowl. Add the chicken, yogurt, banana, peaches and chives to the potato, and mix together. Spoon into the potato cases, then top with the cheese. Return to the oven for 10 minutes. Serve. SERVES 4

Enchilada

🍅

4 WHEAT TORTILLAS

Sauce

1 tablespoon OLIVE OIL

1 ONION, CHOPPED

1 GARLIC CLOVE, CHOPPED

1 RED CHILI, CHOPPED

1 tablespoon TOMATO PASTE

14-ounce can CHOPPED TOMATOES

1¼ *cups* CHICKEN STOCK

1½ *cups* DICED COOKED CHICKEN

2 SCALLIONS, CHOPPED

1 RED BELL PEPPER, SEEDED AND CHOPPED

1 teaspoon CHILI POWDER

1 AVOCADO, PEELED, PITTED AND DICED

1 cup GRATED CHEDDAR CHEESE

Preheat the oven to 400°F. To make the sauce, heat the oil in a pan, and sauté the onion, garlic and chili for 5 minutes, or until soft. Stir in the tomato paste, canned tomatoes and stock, then simmer for 15 minutes.

Meanwhile, mix together the chicken, scallions, red bell pepper and chili powder. Stir in 3 tablespoons of the sauce and the avocado.

Place the tortillas on a chopping board. Spoon a quarter of the chicken mixture into each tortilla. Roll up and place in an ovenproof dish. Pour the tomato sauce over the top, and sprinkle over the cheese. Bake for 20 minutes. Serve with salad. SERVES 4

TOP: *Twice-Baked Potatoes*
BOTTOM: *Enchilada*

Banana Monsieur

❦

8 SLICES WHITE BREAD
⅓ cup SOFTENED BUTTER
4 SLICES COOKED HAM
6 ounces STILTON CHEESE
2 small BANANAS, SLICED

Spread one side of each slice of bread generously with butter. Place a slice of ham on the unbuttered side of 4 slices of bread. Top with the Stilton and banana. Place the remaining bread on top, buttered side outward. Cut in half on the diagonal to form triangles.

Melt the remaining butter in a skillet, and fry the sandwiches for 6 minutes, turning once. Serve immediately.

SERVES 4

Sausage Pasties

❦

1 tablespoon OLIVE OIL
1 pound HERB SAUSAGES
1 tablespoon ALL-PURPOSE FLOUR
⅔ cup MILK
1 GREEN EATING APPLE, CORED AND CHOPPED
1 tablespoon CHOPPED FRESH THYME
1 pound PREPARED PLAIN PASTRY DOUGH
BEATEN EGG, TO GLAZE

Heat the oil in a skillet, and cook the sausages, turning frequently, for 15 minutes, or until cooked through. Remove from the skillet, and slice. Return the sausages to the skillet. Add the flour, and cook for 1 minute. Stir in the milk, then add the apple and thyme. Let cool.

Preheat the oven to 375°F. Roll out the pastry on a lightly floured counter to a 12 × 20-inch rectangle. Cut out 8 equal rectangles. Place some filling in the center of each rectangle, and brush the edges of the dough with egg. Fold the dough to meet in the center and form a seam, then pinch and seal. Place the pasties on a lightly oiled baking sheet, and brush with egg. Bake for 20–25 minutes.

SERVES 8

TOP: *Banana Monsieur*
BOTTOM: *Sausage Pasties*

Desserts

Fruits really come into their own element in this chapter. Being so versatile, they are used to make a variety of desserts. Some are quick to prepare, while others are more elaborate and suitable for special occasions.

Gooseberry Cheesecake

Base

6 ounces OAT COOKIES

⅓ *cup* UNSALTED BUTTER

Filling

2 *cups* DESSERT GOOSEBERRIES, TOPPED AND TAILED

½ *cup* SUPERFINE SUGAR

2 *tablespoons* WATER

1½ *cups* FULL-FAT CREAM CHEESE

2 EGGS, SEPARATED

4 *teaspoons* POWDERED GELATIN

1¼ *cups* HEAVY CREAM

To decorate

HEAVY CREAM

DESSERT GOOSEBERRIES, MOISTENED AND DIPPED IN SUPERFINE SUGAR

FRESH MINT SPRIGS

Put the cookies into a food processor, and work for 30 seconds to make fine crumbs. Melt the butter in a pan, then stir the crumbs into the butter, mixing well. Press into the base of an 8-inch springform pan. Chill.

Put the gooseberries into a saucepan with the sugar and water. Cook for 5 minutes until soft. Let cool slightly, then put into a food processor and purée for 30 seconds. Mix together the cream cheese and egg yolks in a bowl, and stir in the gooseberry purée. Dissolve the gelatin in hot water, and let cool slightly. Whip the cream until peaking, then stir into the gooseberry mixture. Stir in the gelatin. Beat the egg whites until stiff, and fold into the mixture. Pour the mixture onto the chilled base, return to the refrigerator and chill for another 3 hours, or until set. Remove the cheesecake from the pan, and place on a serving plate. Decorate with piped whipped cream, gooseberries and mint.   SERVES 8

RIGHT: Gooseberry Cheesecake

Berry Savarin

☙

2 cups WHITE BREAD FLOUR
pinch of SALT
4 teaspoons DRIED YEAST
6 tablespoons TEPID MILK
2 tablespoons SUPERFINE SUGAR
4 EGGS
½ cup SOFTENED UNSALTED BUTTER
4 tablespoons LIGHT CORN SYRUP
2 tablespoons DARK RUM
4 tablespoons WATER
1½ pounds MIXED BERRIES, SUCH AS
BLACKCURRANTS, REDCURRANTS,
RASPBERRIES, BLACKBERRIES AND
STRAWBERRIES
SUPERFINE SUGAR, TO SPRINKLE

Sift the flour into a bowl, and add the salt. Stir the yeast into the milk. Add ½ teaspoon sugar, and let sit for 15 minutes. Mix the yeast mixture into the flour with the remaining sugar, eggs and butter. Beat well for 5 minutes. Grease an 8-inch ring mold, and spoon the mixture into it. Cover and let rise in a warm place until doubled in size.

Preheat the oven to 400°F. Bake the savarin for 20 minutes, or until a skewer inserted in the center comes out clean. Invert onto a wire rack with a baking sheet underneath. Prick the savarin all over.

Warm the syrup and rum in a pan with the water. Pour over the savarin, and let sit for 20 minutes. Transfer the savarin onto a serving plate, and fill the center with the fruit. Sprinkle with superfine sugar, and serve.   SERVES 8

Lime Syllabub

☙

⅔ cup DRY WHITE WINE
⅓ cup SUPERFINE SUGAR
grated peel and juice of 2 LIMES
1¼ cups HEAVY CREAM
4 MACAROONS, BROKEN

To decorate
LIME ZEST
MINT

Mix the wine and sugar with the lime peel and juice. Cover and let infuse for 3 hours. Whip the cream until peaking, and add the infusion gradually, beating until the mixture holds its shape.

Line the bottom of 4 dessert glasses with the macaroons, and spoon the mixture on top. Chill for 2 hours. Decorate and serve.   SERVES 4

TOP: Berry Savarin
BOTTOM: Lime Syllabub

Melon Mousse

❦

1¼ *cups* HEAVY CREAM
1¼ *cups* CREME FRAICHE
2 EGGS, SEPARATED
1 *envelope* POWDERED GELATIN
1 CHARENTAIS MELON, SEEDED, PEELED
AND CHOPPED
2 *tablespoons* SIFTED CONFECTIONERS' SUGAR
½ *teaspoon* GROUND GINGER
FRESH MINT SPRIGS, TO DECORATE

Whip the cream until peaking, then add the crème fraîche and egg yolks. Dissolve the gelatin in hot water, and let cool slightly. Put the chopped melon flesh into a food processor, and purée for 30 seconds. Stir into the cream with the sugar and ginger. Stir in the gelatin.

Beat the egg whites until peaking, then fold into the mixture. Spoon into a 4-pint jelly or mousse mold and chill for 3 hours, or until set.

Dip the mold into hot water, then invert onto a serving plate. Remove the mold, and decorate the mousse with mint. Serve immediately. SERVES 4

Pavlova

❦

3 EGG WHITES
1 *teaspoon* CORNSTARCH
1 *teaspoon* VINEGAR
¾ *cup* SUPERFINE SUGAR
1¼ *cups* HEAVY CREAM
2 PASSION FRUIT
2 MANGOES, PEELED
FRESH MINT SPRIGS, TO DECORATE

Preheat the oven to 325°F. Beat the egg whites until stiff. Mix together the cornstarch and vinegar. Beat into the egg whites with half of the sugar, then fold in the remaining sugar.

Lay a piece of baking parchment on a baking sheet. Draw an 8-inch round onto the parchment, and spoon on the meringue. Bake the pavlova for 1 hour, then let cool.

Whip the cream until peaking. Halve the passion fruit, and scoop the seeds into the cream. Spoon onto the meringue. Chop the mango flesh, and spoon on top of the cream. Decorate with mint sprigs. SERVES 8

TOP: Melon Mousse
BOTTOM: Pavlova

Ice Cream Bombe

☙

3¾ *cups* HEAVY CREAM
6 *tablespoons* MILK
generous ¾ *cup* SIFTED CONFECTIONERS' SUGAR
2 *pounds* WATERMELON, PEELED AND CHOPPED
4 KIWI FRUIT, PEELED AND CHOPPED

To decorate
KIWI FRUIT, SLICED
FRESH MINT SPRIGS

Whip the cream and milk in a bowl until stiff, then add the confectioners' sugar. Put the watermelon into a food processor, and work for 30 seconds, or until puréed. Transfer to a bowl. Purée the kiwi fruit for 30 seconds in a food processor, and transfer to a separate bowl. Add two-thirds of the cream mixture to the watermelon, and stir well to mix. Transfer to a freezerproof container, and freeze for 45 minutes.

Put the remaining cream mixture into the bowl with the kiwi fruit, and stir well to mix. Transfer to a freezerproof container, and freeze for 45 minutes.

Transfer the ice cream to separate bowls, and beat until smooth. Return to separate containers, and freeze for another 2 hours, or until firm. Remove the water melon ice cream from the freezer, and let sit for 20 minutes. Scoop the watermelon ice cream into the bottom and sides of a chilled bombe mold, leaving a hollow in the center. Return to the freezer for 1 hour.

Meanwhile, remove the kiwi ice cream from the freezer 20 minutes before using. Scoop into the center of the watermelon ice cream, and return to the freezer for another hour, or until completely frozen. Dip the mold into hot water, and invert onto a serving plate to unmold the ice cream bombe. Decorate with sliced kiwi fruit and mint sprigs.

SERVES 6

RIGHT: Ice Cream Bombe

Frudités

❦

½ HONEYDEW MELON, PEELED, SEEDED
    AND CHOPPED
1 PEAR, PEELED, CORED AND SLICED
1 RED EATING APPLE, CORED AND SLICED
1 RUBY GRAPEFRUIT, PEELED AND CUT
    INTO SEGMENTS
1½ cups STRAWBERRIES, WASHED
1 tablespoon SUPERFINE SUGAR

Cream
⅔ cup HEAVY CREAM, WHIPPED
⅔ cup CREME FRAICHE
1 tablespoon CONFECTIONERS' SUGAR, SIFTED
2 PASSION FRUIT

Arrange the prepared fruit on a platter. Sprinkle with superfine sugar. Mix together the cream, crème fraîche and sugar, scooping the passion fruit seeds into the cream. Serve with the frudités.   SERVES 6

Tropical Trifle

❦

4 ounces GINGER CAKE
2 tablespoons BANANA LIQUEUR
1 BANANA
1 KIWI FRUIT, PEELED
1 MANGO, PEELED
6 LYCHEES, PEELED AND HALVED
1¼ cups HEAVY CREAM
    GROUND CHERRIES, TO DECORATE

Custard
2 EGGS
1 tablespoon SUPERFINE SUGAR
1¼ cups MILK
few drops of ALMOND EXTRACT

Cut the ginger cake into slices, and place in the bottom of a serving bowl. Spoon on the liqueur, and let sit. Place the banana and kiwi on top of the ginger cake. Slice the mango from around the pit. Place the mango and lychees in the bowl.

To make the custard, beat together the eggs and sugar with 3 tablespoons of the milk. Heat the remaining milk in a pan, and bring to a boil. Remove from the heat, and pour onto the egg mixture, stirring constantly. Strain into the pan, and return to the heat, cooking over a low heat and stirring until the mixture thickens enough to coat the back of the spoon. Do not let it boil. Stir in the almond extract. Let cool completely. When cool, pour the custard over the fruit, and chill for 1 hour.

Whip the cream until peaking, then spoon onto the top of the chilled custard. Decorate with a few ground cherries and serve.   SERVES 8

Top: Frudités
Bottom: Tropical Trifle

Citrus Brandy Baskets

❧

Baskets

¼ *cup* UNSALTED BUTTER
¼ *cup* GOLDEN GRANULATED SUGAR
¼ *cup* LIGHT CORN SYRUP
½ *cup* ALL-PURPOSE FLOUR
1 *teaspoon* GROUND GINGER
1 *teaspoon* LEMON JUICE

Mousse

⅔ *cup* HEAVY CREAM
1 EGG, SEPARATED
grated zest of 1 ORANGE
1 ORANGE, PEELED AND CUT INTO SEGMENTS
2 *tablespoons* ORANGE JUICE
½ *envelope* POWDERED GELATIN
2 *tablespoons* SIFTED CONFECTIONERS' SUGAR
GRATED ORANGE ZEST, TO DECORATE

Preheat the oven to 325°F. To make the brandy snap baskets, put the butter into a pan with the sugar and syrup. Melt over a low heat, stirring constantly. Sift the flour and ginger together, then add to the mixture with the lemon juice. Mix well.

Spoon the mixture into 4 rounds on a greased baking sheet, spacing well apart. Bake for 8 minutes. Remove from the oven, and let sit for 1 minute. Grease the outside of 4 cups lightly, and invert on the counter. Remove the brandy snaps from the baking sheet, and mold around the cups, fluting. Let sit until firm, then remove from the cups.

Meanwhile, make the mousse. Whip the cream until peaking, and stir in the egg yolk. Add the orange zest, juice and chopped flesh. Dissolve the gelatin in hot water, and let cool slightly. Stir into the orange mixture with the sugar. Beat the egg white until peaking, then fold into the mousse. Spoon into a bowl, and chill for 2 hours, or until half-set. Spoon the mousse mixture into the brandy snap baskets, then return to the refrigerator to chill until firm. Decorate with orange segments and grated zest, and serve.   SERVES 4

RIGHT: Citrus Brandy Baskets

Puddings, Cakes & Bakes

Some favorite recipes from around the world are included in this chapter, making use of the many different fruits now available internationally in a selection of recipes ranging from cakes and breads to pies.

Cherry Clafoutis

3 cups RIPE CHERRIES, PITTED
4 tablespoons CHERRY BRANDY
¾ cup ALL-PURPOSE FLOUR
⅓ cup SOFT BROWN SUGAR
3 eggs, BEATEN
1¼ cups HEAVY CREAM
4 tablespoons MELTED UNSALTED BUTTER
SIFTED CONFECTIONERS' SUGAR, TO DREDGE

Put the cherries into a bowl, and sprinkle with 2 tablespoons of the cherry brandy. Let sit for 1 hour. Sift the flour into a bowl, and stir in the sugar. Beat in the eggs and cream gradually to make a smooth batter. Drain the cherries, reserving the juice. Add the juice and butter to the batter. Preheat the oven to 400°F.

Arrange the cherries in an ovenproof dish, then pour over the batter. Bake for 30–35 minutes, or until risen and set. Dust with confectioners' sugar, and sprinkle with the remaining cherry brandy. SERVES 6

Peach Dumplings

4 RIPE PEACHES
½ cup GROUND ALMONDS
2 tablespoons BRANDY
1 pound PREPARED SWEET PASTRY DOUGH
BEATEN EGG, TO GLAZE

Preheat the oven to 375°F. Rinse the peaches, halve and remove the pits. Combine the ground almonds and brandy, and spoon into the center of the peaches; then place the two peach halves together.

Roll out the dough to a 20-inch square. Cut out 4 matching squares from the dough, and brush the edges with beaten egg. Place a peach in the center of each square, and wrap the pastry around the peach, encasing it completely and sealing at the base. Decorate with leaves made from the dough trimmings and placed on top of each dumpling. Brush with beaten egg, and bake for 30 minutes. Serve with cream. SERVES 4

TOP: Cherry Clafoutis
BOTTOM: Peach Dumplings

Chocolate Pear Pudding

☙

2 PEARS, PEELED AND CORED
2 tablespoons BROWN SUGAR
4 tablespoons WATER
½ cup UNSALTED BUTTER
½ cup SUPERFINE SUGAR
2 EGGS, BEATEN
1½ cups SELF-RISING FLOUR
2 squares DARK CHOCOLATE
¼ cup CHOPPED, SHELLED PECAN NUTS
ANGELICA, TO DECORATE

Preheat the oven to 350°F. Halve the pears, and put into a pan with the brown sugar and water. Poach gently for 5 minutes. Remove the pears, and place in the bottom of a greased and bottom-lined 8-inch cake pan. Boil the syrup in a pan for 3 minutes, and pour over the pears.

Beat the butter and sugar until white and creamy. Add the eggs gradually, and fold in the flour. Melt the chocolate over a pan of boiling water, then stir into the flour mixture with the pecan nuts. Spoon the mixture over the pears.

Bake the pudding for 1 hour, or until a skewer inserted in the center comes out clean. Invert the pudding onto a serving plate. Decorate with angelica, and serve with custard or cream.

SERVES 4

Cherry Strudel

☙

8 ounces FILO PASTRY
2 tablespoons MELTED UNSALTED BUTTER
4 tablespoons GROUND ALMONDS
1½ pounds RIPE CHERRIES, RINSED AND PITTED
¼ cup SUPERFINE SUGAR
1 cup CHOPPED BLANCHED ALMONDS

Preheat the oven to 400°F. Lay 1 sheet of filo pastry on a counter. Brush with melted butter, and lay another sheet on top. Repeat until all the filo pastry is used. Sprinkle over the ground almonds, then lay the cherries at one end of the filo pastry. Top with the sugar and chopped almonds, then roll up like a jelly roll. Fold in the edges, and place on a lightly greased baking sheet. Shape the roll into a horseshoe. Brush with melted butter, and bake for 20 minutes. Reduce the oven temperature to 350°F, and cook for an additional 10 minutes. Remove from the oven, dust with confectioners' sugar, and serve.

SERVES 8

TOP: *Chocolate Pear Pudding*
BOTTOM: *Cherry Strudel*

Blueberry Muffins

☙

2 cups ALL-PURPOSE FLOUR
2 teaspoons BAKING POWDER
½ teaspoon SALT
¼ cup SUPERFINE SUGAR
1 EGG, BEATEN
1¼ cups MILK
¼ cup SOFTENED UNSALTED BUTTER
1 cup BLUEBERRIES, RINSED

Line 2 muffin pans with 12 paper muffin cases. Preheat the oven to 400°F. Sift the flour, baking powder and salt into a bowl, and add the sugar. Make a well in the center of the flour mixture, then add the egg and milk. Beat in the flour and butter gradually; do not overbeat. Add the blueberries. Mix together, and spoon into the prepared cases. Bake for 20 minutes. Serve in the paper cases.

SERVES 12

Orange & Cinnamon Bread

☙

2 cups WHITE BREAD FLOUR
pinch of SALT
2 tablespoons UNSALTED BUTTER
1 teaspoon SUPERFINE SUGAR
⅓ cup GOLDEN RAISINS
⅓ cup RAISINS
2 tablespoons MIXED PEEL
1 teaspoon GROUND CINNAMON
grated zest and juice of 1 ORANGE
1½ teaspoons EASY-BLEND DRIED YEAST
1 small EGG
½ cup TEPID MILK

To decorate
CONFECTIONERS' SUGAR
GRATED ORANGE ZEST

Grease an 8-inch deep round cake pan. Sift the flour and salt into a bowl, then rub in the butter until the mixture resembles breadcrumbs. Stir in the sugar, dried fruit, mixed peel, cinnamon, orange zest and juice, then stir in the easy-blend dried yeast. Add the egg and milk to the mixture, and mix together to form a smooth dough. Knead on a lightly floured counter for 10 minutes. Place in a clean bowl, and cover with a clean damp dishcloth. Let the mixture rise in a warm place for about 1 hour, or until doubled in size.

Remove the dough from the bowl, and knead on a lightly floured counter for 2–3 minutes. Divide into 6 equal pieces, and shape into balls. Place one ball in the center of the greased pan and arrange the remaining 5 around the outside. Cover with a clean damp dishcloth, and leave until doubled in size.

Preheat the oven to 400°F. Bake the loaf for 45 minutes, or until the bottom of the loaf sounds hollow when tapped. Invert onto a wire rack, and let cool. Dust the top with confectioners' sugar, and decorate with grated orange zest.

SERVES 6

TOP: Blueberry Muffins
BOTTOM: Orange & Cinnamon Bread

Tarte Tatin

❦

Pastry Dough
2 cups ALL-PURPOSE FLOUR
¼ cup SUPERFINE SUGAR
¾ cup UNSALTED BUTTER
1 EGG YOLK
2 teaspoons WATER

Topping
⅔ cup SOFT BROWN SUGAR
2 pounds EATING APPLES, PEELED AND SLICED
¼ cup MELTED UNSALTED BUTTER

Sift the flour into a bowl. Add the superfine sugar, and make a well in the center. Put the butter and egg yolks in the center with the water, and bring the mixture together with your hands to form a soft dough. Wrap in plastic wrap, then chill for 1 hour.

To make the topping, sprinkle 2 tablespoons of the brown sugar over the bottom of an 8-inch cake pan. Arrange the sliced apples over the bottom of the pan, layering with the remaining sugar. Drizzle over the melted butter. Place the pan over a low heat for about 20 minutes until the sugar melts and begins to caramelize. Remove the pan from the heat.

Preheat the oven to 425°F. Roll out the dough on a lightly floured counter to an 8-inch round. Place the dough on top of the apples, and bake for 20 minutes. Invert onto a serving plate and serve with cream. SERVES 6

Rhubarb Cobbler

❦

1½ cups SELF-RISING FLOUR
⅓ cup UNSALTED BUTTER
⅔ cup MILK
2 pounds RHUBARB, TRIMMED AND CHOPPED
½ teaspoon GROUND GINGER
1 tablespoon WATER
¼ cup SUPERFINE SUGAR
⅔ cup HEAVY CREAM
1 tablespoon SOFT BROWN SUGAR

Preheat the oven to 425°F. Sift the flour into a bowl, then rub in ¼ cup of the butter until the mixture resembles breadcrumbs. Stir in the milk to make a smooth dough, then roll out on a lightly floured counter. Stamp out eight 2-inch rounds, then place the scones on a greased baking sheet, and bake for 10 minutes.

Meanwhile, put the rhubarb into a pan with the ginger, water and superfine sugar. Cook over a low heat for 10 minutes or until soft. Transfer to a flameproof dish.

Split the scones, and spread with the remaining butter. Arrange around the edge of the dish. Pour the cream into the center, then sprinkle the brown sugar over. Cook under a hot broiler for 3–4 minutes. Serve. SERVES 4

TOP: Tarte Tatin
BOTTOM: Rhubarb Cobbler

Deep Apple Pie

🍎

2½ cups ALL-PURPOSE FLOUR

pinch of SALT

⅔ cup UNSALTED BUTTER

¼ cup FRESHLY GRATED CHEDDAR CHEESE

4 tablespoons WATER

2 pounds COOKING APPLES, PEELED, CORED AND SLICED

1 teaspoon GROUND CINNAMON

⅓ cup GOLDEN RAISINS

⅓ cup SUPERFINE SUGAR

knob of BUTTER

1 EGG, BEATEN, TO GLAZE

Sift the flour and salt into a bowl. Rub in the butter until the mixture resembles bread crumbs. Stir in the cheese, and bind the mixture with the water to form a smooth dough. Wrap in plastic wrap, then chill for 30 minutes.

Preheat the oven to 400°F. Roll out half of the dough to fit a 9-inch diameter deep pie dish. Line the dish with the dough. Roll out the remaining dough for the lid. Place the apples in the bottom of the pie dish with the cinnamon, golden raisins and sugar, then top with the butter.

Dampen the edges of the dough with the beaten egg, and place the lid on top. Trim the edges and pinch together. Crimp the rim with a fork. Brush the top of the pie with beaten egg, and make a small hole in the center. Decorate with any dough trimmings, and bake for 20 minutes. Reduce the oven temperature to 350°F, and bake for an additional 20 minutes. Serve with fresh cream.

SERVES 6

Baked Orange Cheesecake

🍎

½ cup UNSALTED BUTTER

8 ounces GRAHAM CRACKERS

1 pound FULL-FAT CREAM CHEESE

3 EGGS, BEATEN

¾ cup SUPERFINE SUGAR

grated peel and juice of 1 ORANGE

1¼ cups SOUR CREAM

3 KUMQUATS, SLICED

⅓ cup WATER

Preheat the oven to 350°F. Melt the butter in a pan. Put the crackers into a food processor, and blend for 30 seconds to make fine crumbs. Stir into the butter, then press into the bottom and sides of an 8-inch loose-bottomed pan. Bake for 10 minutes. Beat together the cheese and eggs, and ½ cup of the sugar. Add the orange peel and juice, and pour into the pan. Bake for 1 hour, or until firm. Remove from the oven. Increase the temperature to 425°F.

Mix together 2 tablespoons of the sugar and the sour cream. Spread over the top of the cheesecake, and return to the oven for 8 minutes.

Meanwhile, put the kumquats, the remaining sugar and the water in a pan. Poach for 5 minutes, drain well and let cool. Arrange on top of the cheesecake, and remove from the pan. Let cool and serve.

SERVES 8

TOP: Deep Apple Pie

BOTTOM: Baked Orange Cheesecake

Berry Charlotte

🍎

1 pound BLACKBERRIES, RINSED

1 pound COOKING APPLES, PEELED AND CORED

grated zest of 1 ORANGE

2 tablespoons ORANGE JUICE

1 cup SOFT BROWN SUGAR

6 tablespoons GROUND ALMONDS

1 medium loaf WHITE BREAD

½ cup MELTED UNSALTED BUTTER

1 EGG, BEATEN

BLACKBERRIES AND LEAVES, TO DECORATE

Preheat the oven to 375°F. Grease a 3-pint charlotte mold lightly. Put the blackberries into a pan. Slice the apples thickly, then add to the pan with the orange zest and juice. Simmer for 10 minutes. Add the sugar and ground almonds.

Cut the bread into ½-inch thick slices, and remove the crusts. Trim 2 slices to fit the bottom of the mold, and brush both sides with melted butter. Place in the bottom of the mold. Reserving 2 slices for the top, cut the remaining slices to fit the sides of the mold. Dip into the melted butter to coat both sides, then arrange tightly in the mold, overlapping. Brush the joins with beaten egg. Spoon the fruit mixture into the center, and top with the reserved bread. Brush with the remaining butter and egg. Bake for 1 hour. Remove from the oven, and invert onto a serving plate. Decorate with blackberries and leaves, and serve with custard. SERVES 4

Banana Cake

🍎

¾ cup UNSALTED BUTTER

1 cup SUPERFINE SUGAR

3 EGGS, SEPARATED

3 small BANANAS

⅔ cup SOUR CREAM

2 cups SELF-RISING FLOUR

½ cup GOLDEN RAISINS

grated zest of 1 LEMON

SLICED BANANA, TO DECORATE

Frosting

½ cup FULL-FAT CREAM CHEESE

½ cup SIFTED CONFECTIONERS' SUGAR

Grease and line an 8-inch round cake pan. Preheat the oven to 350°F. Beat the butter and sugar until white and creamy, then beat in the egg yolks gradually. Mash the bananas, and stir into the mixture with the sour cream. Add the flour, golden raisins and lemon. Beat the egg whites until peaking, and fold into the mixture. Spoon the mixture into the pan, and level the surface. Bake for 1 hour, or until a skewer inserted in the center comes out clean. Remove from the oven. Let cool in the pan for 5 minutes, then invert onto a wire rack to cool completely.

Meanwhile, mix together the cream cheese and confectioners' sugar. Spread over the top of the cooled cake, and decorate with banana slices. SERVES 12

TOP: Berry Charlotte

BOTTOM: Banana Cake

Preserves

Fruits are ideal for preserving, whether in the form of jams, bottled in alcohol or as a delicious fruit chutney to be eaten with cold meats and savory snacks, to be enjoyed all year round.

Lemon & Lime Curd

½ cup BUTTER
1¼ cups GRANULATED SUGAR
4 EGGS
grated zest and juice of 2 LEMONS
grated zest and juice of 2 LIMES

Melt the butter in a double boiler, or in a bowl over a pan of hot water. Add the sugar, eggs and lemon and lime zests and juices. Cook over a low heat without boiling until the mixture thickens enough to coat the back of a spoon. Pour into warmed, sterilized glass jars, cover and seal. Use within 2 weeks.

MAKES 1½ POUNDS

Rumtopf

MIXED FRUITS, SUCH AS STRAWBERRIES, CHERRIES, PEACHES, RASPBERRIES, PLUMS AND CURRANTS

SUPERFINE SUGAR

DARK RUM

Wash the rumtopf jar thoroughly in soapy water. Rinse and dry thoroughly. Rinse the fruit gently and pat dry. Halve the peaches and plums, then remove the pits. Pit the cherries, and remove the currants from the stalks. Measure the fruit, and spread it out on a plate. You will need half the volume of the fruit in sugar to sprinkle over the fruit. Let the fruit sit for 1 hour, and then transfer to the rumtopf jar. Pour on enough rum to cover the fruit completely.

Place a clean saucer on top to submerge the fruit. Cover tightly with a lid, and store in a cool place until ready to add more fruit.

Repeat until the rumtopf jar is full, adding more rum if necessary. Store until required.

Top: Lemon & Lime Curd
Bottom: Rumtopf

Gooseberry & Rhubarb Jam

🍎

1¼ *pounds* RHUBARB, CHOPPED
1½ *pounds* GOOSEBERRIES, TOPPED AND TAILED
3 *pounds* SUPERFINE SUGAR
juice of 1 LEMON
1¼ *cups* WATER
knob of BUTTER

Put the rhubarb, gooseberries, sugar, lemon juice and water into a large preserving pan. Simmer for 30 minutes until pulpy. Bring to a boil, and boil rapidly for 20 minutes. Test for a set. Remove from the heat. Add the butter to remove the scum. Pour into warm sterilized glass jars, cover and store. MAKES 4 POUNDS

Mixed Berry Jam

🍎

3 *pounds* MIXED SOFT FRUITS, SUCH AS BLACKBERRIES, LOGANBERRIES, STRAWBERRIES, REDCURRANTS AND BLACKCURRANTS, WASHED AND HULLED AS REQUIRED
⅔ *cup* WATER
3 *pounds* GRANULATED SUGAR
knob of BUTTER

Put the prepared fruits into a large saucepan with the water. Bring to a boil, then reduce the heat, cover and simmer. Remove from the heat, and stir in the sugar until it has dissolved.

Return the pan to the heat, and bring to a boil. Boil rapidly for 15 minutes, or until setting point is reached. Remove from the heat, and stir in the butter to remove the scum. Pour into warmed, sterilized glass jars, cover and store. MAKES 5 POUNDS

Mango Jam

🍎

8 *ripe* MANGOES, PEELED, PITTED AND CHOPPED
peel and juice of 2 LEMONS
1 *cup* WATER
3 *pounds* SUPERFINE SUGAR
knob of BUTTER

Put the fruit and lemon juice into a preserving pan. Cut the lemon peel into strips, and put into a cheesecloth bag. Tie and add to the pan with the water. Bring to a boil, reduce the heat and simmer for 30 minutes, uncovered. Remove the bag from the jam, then remove the pan from the heat. Stir in the sugar until it has dissolved. Return the pan to the heat, then bring to a boil and boil rapidly for 15 minutes. Add the butter to remove the scum. Let sit for 15 minutes. Pour into warmed, sterilized glass jars. Cover and store.

MAKES 4 POUNDS

TOP: Gooseberry & Rhubarb Jam (left); Mixed Berry Jam (right)
BOTTOM: Mango Jam

Three Fruit Marmalade

2 GRAPEFRUIT
4 LEMONS
2 ORANGES
6 *pints* WATER
6 *pounds* GRANULATED SUGAR

Halve and juice the fruits, reserving the seeds. Remove the pith and discard. Cut the fruit peel into thin strips. Put the peel, fruit juice and water into a pan. Put the seeds in a piece of cheesecloth, tie and add to the pan. Bring to a boil, then reduce the heat to a simmer, and cook slowly for about 2 hours.

Squeeze the cheesecloth bag to release the liquid, remove and discard. Stir the sugar into the mixture until dissolved. Bring the marmalade to a boil, and boil rapidly until setting point is reached. Let sit for 1 hour, and pour into warmed, sterilized jars. Seal and label.

MAKES 8 POUNDS

Fruits in Brandy

6 KIWI FRUIT, PEELED
1 MANGO
1½ *cups* SUPERFINE SUGAR
1¼ *cups* WATER
4 PEACHES, HALVED, PITTED AND SLICED
⅔ *cup* BRANDY

Quarter the kiwi fruit. Peel the mango, remove the flesh from around the pit and slice. Dissolve ½ cup of the sugar in the water. Add the fruit, and poach for 5 minutes. Remove from the heat and drain, reserving the syrup and the fruit. Arrange the fruit in sterilized jars.

Add the remaining sugar to the syrup, and put over a low heat to dissolve slowly. Bring to a boil, and boil rapidly until a temperature of 230°F is reached. Remove from the heat, and let cool. Stir the brandy in, then pour over the fruit. Cover and store for 3 months.

MAKES 3 POUNDS

TOP: *Three Fruit Marmalade*
BOTTOM: *Fruits in Brandy*

Fruit Chutney

❦

1 pound COOKING APPLES, PEELED, CORED AND SLICED

3 ripe PEACHES, PEELED, PITTED AND CHOPPED

2 large ONIONS, CHOPPED

1⅓ cups GOLDEN RAISINS

4 cups BROWN SUGAR

2 GARLIC CLOVES, CRUSHED

4 teaspoons SALT

2 teaspoons GROUND GINGER

2 teaspoons PREPARED MUSTARD

1 tablespoon GROUND CORIANDER

2½ pints MALT VINEGAR

Put all the ingredients into a large preserving pan. Bring to a boil slowly. Reduce the heat and simmer, uncovered, for 3 hours, stirring occasionally.

Sterilize the jars, then dry. Spoon the mixture into the jars while warm. Cover with a vinegar-proof top and store.   MAKES 1 POUND

Apple Cheese

❦

1½ pounds COOKING APPLES

1 CINNAMON STICK

1 teaspoon CLOVES

2 cups, per 2½ cups of fruit purée SUPERFINE SUGAR

Quarter and core the apples, and chop the flesh. Put into a large pan with the cinnamon stick and cloves. Add just enough water to cover, then cover the pan, and simmer

for about 1 hour, or until the fruit is really soft. Remove the cloves and cinnamon stick, then press the fruit through a strainer into a bowl.

Return to a clean pan, adding the required amount of sugar. Heat gently, stirring until the sugar has dissolved. Bring to a boil and boil rapidly, stirring frequently, for 40 minutes, or until really thick. Pour into warmed, sterilized jars, and let set.   MAKES 2½ CUPS

Peach & Ginger Jam

❦

4 pounds RIPE PEACHES

2 LEMONS

¼ cup PEELED AND CHOPPED GINGERROOT

1 cup WATER

3 pounds SUPERFINE SUGAR

knob of BUTTER

1¼ cups COMMERCIAL PECTIN

Skin, pit and chop the peaches. Reserve the pits. Halve the lemons, and squeeze the juice. Cut the lemon peel into strips, then put into a cheesecloth bag with the ginger and peach pits. Put the peaches, lemon juice and

bag into a preserving pan with the water. Bring to a boil, then simmer for 30 minutes until the peaches are tender. Remove the bag. Remove the pan from the heat, and stir in the sugar until dissolved. Add the butter, and return to the heat. Bring to a boil, and boil rapidly for 10 minutes. Remove from the heat, and stir in the pectin. Let the jam sit for 20 minutes. Pour into warmed, sterilized jars. Cover and store.   MAKES 4 POUNDS

TOP: Fruit Chutney (left); Apple Cheese (right)
BOTTOM: Peach & Ginger Jam

Index